SHAPES

Science Experiences

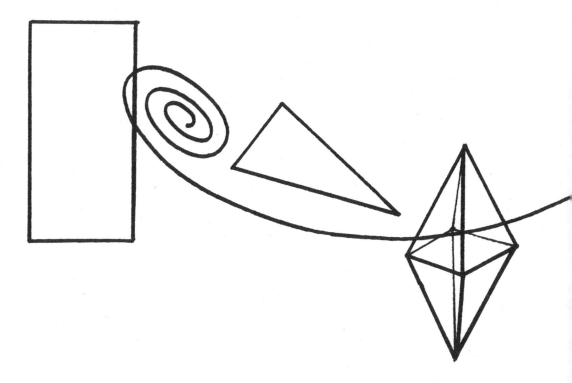

FRANKLIN WATTS, INC.
575 Lexington Avenue · New York, N. Y. 10022

SHAPES

Written and illustrated by

Jeanne Bendick

SBN 531-01433-9

Library of Congress Catalog Card Number: 68-11889
© Copyright 1968 by Jeanne Bendick
Printed in the United States of America by The Garrison Corp.

6 7 8 9 10

SHAPES

This is a shape

and this is a shape.

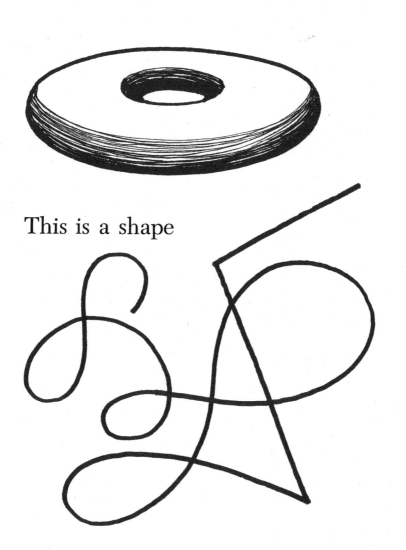

This is a shape

6

and this is a shape.

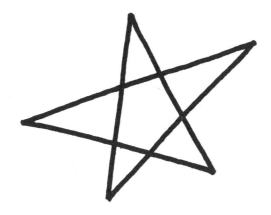

If you take a pencil
and write your name,

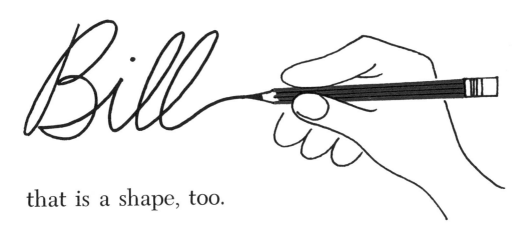

that is a shape, too.

All around you, every day, you see shapes —
the shapes of faces,

the shapes of buildings,

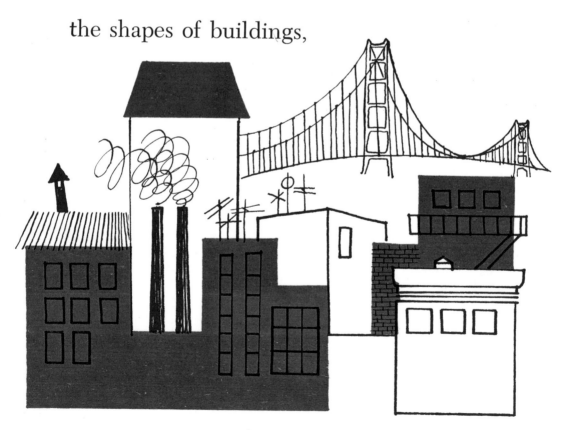

the shapes of cups and plates and cans and bottles and boxes,

the shapes of trees.

You see shapes that tell you things —

the shapes of signs
and the shapes of letters
and the shapes of numerals.

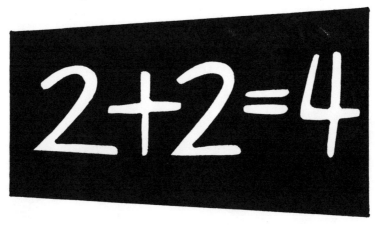

You see beautiful shapes,
like
snowflakes

and
soaring
sea gulls.

And you see some shapes
that are not as pleasant to
look at.

Every shape has something special about it.
You can tell about it.
You can call it by a name.
We call this shape a

Sphere.
(pronounced *sfeer*).

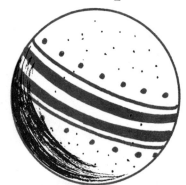

A rubber ball is a sphere.

An orange is a sphere.

A ball of yarn is a sphere.

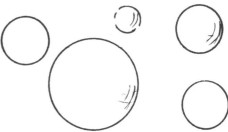

Soap bubbles are
spheres,
and so are
raindrops.

Round shapes that take up
room in space are called

Spheres.

When you say that something is a sphere,
you are telling the special thing about it.
A sphere is round all around.

WHAT DO YOU THINK?

Is a circle a sphere?
Is it round *all* around?

(If you are not sure, you will find the answer later in the book.)

Shapes in mathematics are exact.
The names of shapes are exact.
They are like the names of people you know.
When you hear somebody's name:

"Tony George"

or "Jill Rice"

or "your teacher,
Miss Warren,"

you know *exactly* what the name means.
It doesn't mean "somebody like Tony
George."
It doesn't mean "maybe Jill Rice."
It doesn't mean "almost Miss Warren."

Once you know the names of shapes, you will always know *exactly* what the shape is when you hear its name.

A SPHERE *always* means "round all around," not "sort of round."

A RIGHT ANGLE *always* means exactly this shape, no matter how it is turned.

A SQUARE *always* means a shape with four right angles and four sides *exactly* the same length, not *almost* the same length.

A CIRCLE *always* means a closed curved line *exactly* this shape, whether it is big or small.

The mathematical names of shapes are *precise*.

But even if you do not know the name of a shape, you can always tell something about it.

You could say that this is squiggly,

and this is jiggly.

Then, when you knew more names for shapes, you could say that the squiggly one was made of

loops

and curves

and the jiggly one was made of straight lines

and angles.

Did you ever think that different shapes can make you feel different ways?

Sharp, steep
mountains
are exciting.

Rounded hills
are peaceful.

Lightning
isn't peaceful.

The ocean can
look rhythmic

or scary,

depending on the shape of the waves.
A face can look

pleasant   or grouchy,

depending on the shape of its mouth.

Some shapes are flat.
You can draw a circle on a piece of paper.

You can write a word *candy*

or a numeral. 2

You can draw
somebody.

Shapes that are flat on paper (or on a blackboard) are called

plane shapes or
plane figures

"Plane" is another name for a flat surface.

This is a plane shape.

This is a plane shape.

This is a plane shape.

This is a plane shape.

You can measure a plane shape in two
directions.
You can measure how long it is.

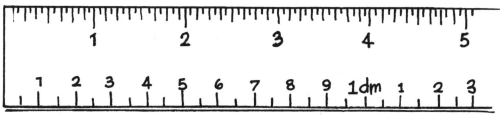

You can measure how wide
it is.
We say that plane shapes
have
two dimensions,

length and width

Suppose you take a pencil and draw something with *one dimension* — length.

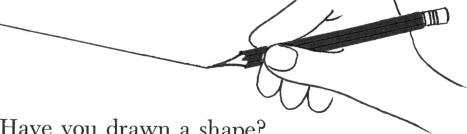

Have you drawn a shape?
You have drawn part of a line.
Whatever part of a line you draw is called a
LINE SEGMENT, which means "a part of a line."
However long you make a line segment, you
can always make it longer. There is no end
to the idea of a line. You could never draw
a whole line, even if you could draw it to
the stars and beyond.

Can you draw something with *no* dimensions?
If you make a dot — the tiniest point — you have drawn something with no dimensions.

You cannot measure how long or how wide it is.

A dot, or point, has no dimensions, but it is something. A line segment is something, too — it is part of a line.

(When you draw arrows at the end of a line segment they mean "This line can go on and on.")

Are points shapes?

Are line segments shapes?

Usually we think of a shape as something with at least two dimensions — length and width.

But could you make a shape with dots?

Could you make a shape with lines?

Certainly. You can draw any plane shapes you want with dots
and lines —
straight lines
and curved lines.

What do you think of, when you think of a curved line?

Some mathematicians say that this is a curve,

and this is a curve,

and even this is a curve.

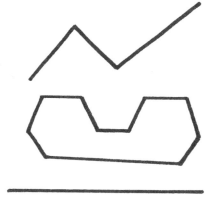

But usually we think of a curve as something like this.

This is an open curve.

A CIRCLE is a closed curve.

An ELLIPSE is a closed curve.

If the line in a closed curve does not cross itself, the curve is a simple curve.

If the line crosses itself, the curve is not a simple one.

If you write a zero, is it a simple or a not-simple curve?

If you write an eight, is it a simple or a not-simple curve?

Many plane figures are called
POLYGONS (poll'-i-gonz).

Polygons are closed plane figures.
They are simple.
They are made of line segments,
joined together.
This is a polygon,

and so is this,

and so is this.

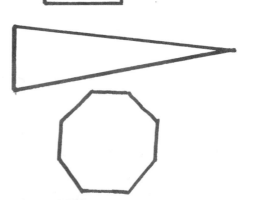

WHAT DO YOU THINK?

Is this a polygon?

It is not closed.
No. It is not simple.

Polygons have sides
and angles.

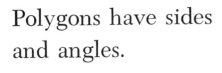

When you see this shape, it means ANGLE.

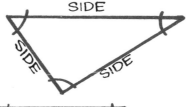

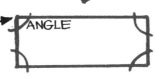

But what is an *angle?*

Line segments that cross,
or *intersect,*   form angles.

The sides of an angle, when
they are not joined
together in a polygon, are
called *rays.* (What does the
arrow at the end of each
ray tell you?)

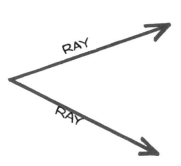

You can draw angles.

You can see angles wher-
ever you look.

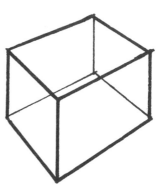

The corners of a box form
angles.

The blades of a pair of
scissors make angles.

So do the branches of a tree.

Where can you see the angles in your room?

31

A clock is a good place to see all kinds of angles.

The hands form new angles as they move.

Sometimes the hands make a right angle.

TRY IT YOURSELF

Can you think of other times when the clock hands form a right angle?

Sometimes the hands make a *straight angle.*

Sometimes the hands make an *acute angle,* which is smaller than a right angle,

or an *obtuse angle,* which is larger than a right angle.

WHAT DO YOU THINK?

Do the hands form an angle when one hand is right on top of the other?

33

Different kinds of angles, joined together, make different kinds of polygons.

Some polygons have beautiful names, almost like singing.

A *triangle.*

A *quadrilateral.*
(kwod-ri-lat'-er-al)

There are many kinds of quadrilaterals —

squares

and *rectangles,*
parallelograms,
(par-a-lel'-o-gramz)
trapeziums,
(tra-pee'-zi-umz)

and *trapezoids.*
(trap'-e-zoidz)

The name of a polygon tells how many sides
it has and how many angles.

"Polygon" means
"many-sided."

A *pentagon.*
(pen'-ta-gon)

DO IT YOURSELF
Count to see what
each name means.

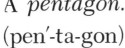

A *hexagon.*
(hek'-sa-gon)

An *octagon.*
(ok'-ta-gon)

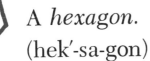

A *heptagon.*
(hep'-ta-gon)

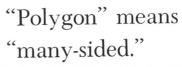

A *nonagon.*
(non'-a-gon)

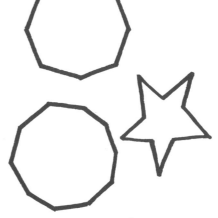

Two *decagons.*
(dek'-a-gonz)

Shapes that have three dimensions in space have beautiful names, too. There are *spheres* and *hemispheres,* (hem'-i-sfeerz)

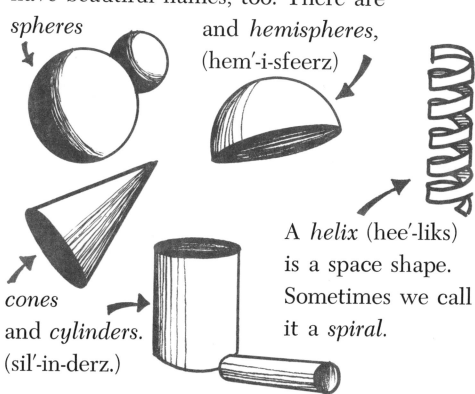

A *helix* (hee'-liks) is a space shape. Sometimes we call it a *spiral.*

cones and *cylinders.* (sil'-in-derz.)

These space shapes have curved surfaces, and maybe plane surfaces too.

WHAT DO YOU THINK?

Which of the shapes on this page has no plane surface?

Some space shapes are formed of only plane surfaces.

These are called POLYHEDRONS (pol-i-hee'-drunz).

"Polyhedron" means "many-faced."

Each plane surface of a polyhedron is called a *face*.

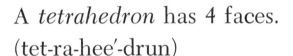

A *tetrahedron* has 4 faces.
(tet-ra-hee'-drun)

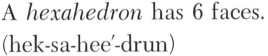

A *hexahedron* has 6 faces.
(hek-sa-hee'-drun)

An *octahedron* has 8 faces.
(ok-ta-hee'-drun)

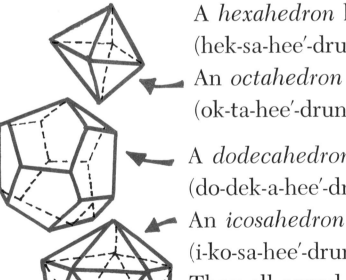

A *dodecahedron* has 12 faces.
(do-dek-a-hee'-drun)

An *icosahedron* has 20 faces.
(i-ko-sa-hee'-drun)

They all sound beautiful!

You can draw a picture of a ball on paper.

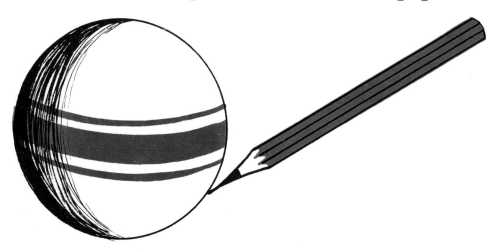

You can draw a picture of a box on paper.

You can draw a mountain

or a bird or a bug

or a candy cane.

But can you draw a *real* ball

or box

or bug

or candy cane?

Can you play with the ball on this page?
Can you put something into the box?
Can the bug fly away?
Can you eat the candy cane?

40

Real balls, boxes, mountains, birds, bugs, and
candy canes take up room in space.
They have *three dimensions,*

**length,
width,
height**

Shapes that have three dimensions are called SPACE SHAPES,
or sometimes SOLID SHAPES. They
have these names whether
they are empty inside or solid
all the way through.

You cannot put a real shape with three dimensions onto a plane surface like a piece of paper, which has only two dimensions.

You can only draw its picture.

You can use plane shapes to draw pictures of space shapes.

With triangles and rectangles, you can draw a house built of cubes and pyramids and other polyhedrons. With circles and lines, you can draw a bunch of balloons, which are spheres on strings.

You can draw a person with any shapes you want.

Can you make actual space shapes, with three dimensions, out of plane shapes, with two dimensions?

Copy this plane figure on another paper. It is three squares wide and four squares long. (You can make your squares as large as you want to.)

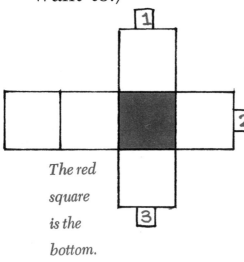

The red square is the bottom.

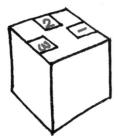

Now cut the figure out. Be sure to leave the tabs for pasting. Fold the squares up, away from the bottom, and paste the tabs. Do you still have a plane shape?

Now you have a shape that takes up space.

44

You can take a sheet of paper and wrap it
into a cone
or a cylinder.

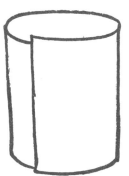

You can twist a strip of paper

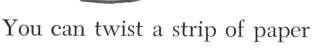

into a helix.

You can make a paper hat
out of a sheet of newspaper.

Is there any space
shape that you cannot
make out of a plane
shape?

You cannot make a sphere.

45

How can you draw space shapes with plane shapes?

How can you build space shapes with plane shapes?

Every space shape has at least one plane shape — or maybe more — that is related to it.

TRY THIS YOURSELF

Can you match these space shapes with their related plane shapes?

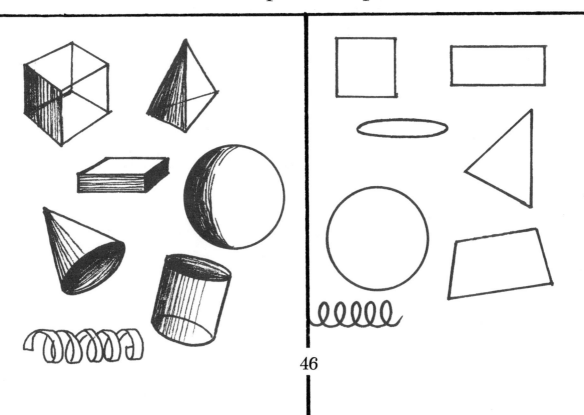

One good way to see
relationships between
space shapes and plane
shapes is to look at
their shadows.

One good way to see relationships between many kinds of things is to look at their shapes.

Learning to look at shapes helps you to *classify* things. Looking at shapes helps you to group things so that you can see what is alike and what is not alike.

You can group things by shape.

You can group the shapes on these pages into sets of

CIRCLES

and TRIANGLES

and QUADRILATERALS

and CURVES

and STARS, which are made of other shapes.

NOW TRY THIS

Can you group the shapes in another way?

Into curves and polygons?

Are there other ways in which you could group these shapes?

There are different ways of classifying things.

Could you group these leaves by shape?

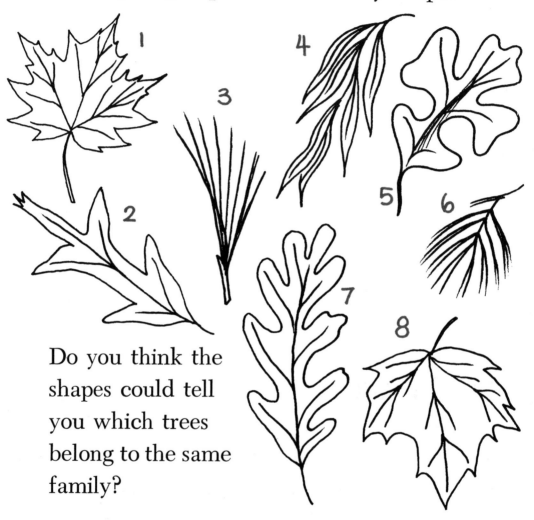

Do you think the shapes could tell you which trees belong to the same family?

1 and 8 are maple leaves. 2, 7, and 5 are oak leaves. 3 and 6 are pine leaves. 4 is a willow leaf.

50

Could you group these seeds by shape?
Could the shapes tell you which seeds would
grow into trees of the same family?

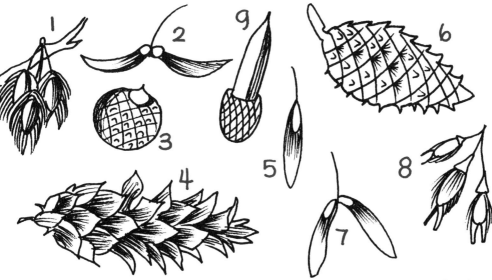

When you are looking at shapes, you look for
what is alike,

and you look for what is different.

You compare shapes to see what is alike and
what is different.

3 and 9 are oak seeds. 2 and 7 are maple seeds.
5 is an ash seed. 4 and 6 are pine cones. 1 and 8 are
elm seeds.

You can see so many things if you know
how to compare shapes.

What words can you use when you are comparing shapes?

You can tell so many things if you know the
words for comparing.

When you compare the
shapes of these bills,
you can see that one is
STRAIGHT and one is
CURVED.

When you compare the
sizes of these acorns,
you can see that one is
BIG and one is SMALL.

When you compare the
shapes of these shells,
you can see that one is
WIDE and one is NARROW.

When you compare the shapes of these toad-stools you can see that one is TALL and one is SHORT. (What else can you see about them?) When you compare these shapes you can see that one is a PLANE SHAPE and one is a SPACE SHAPE.

When you compare these shapes you can see that one is SYMMET-RICAL and one is NOT-SYMMETRICAL.

One has SYMMETRY and one does not have SYMMETRY.

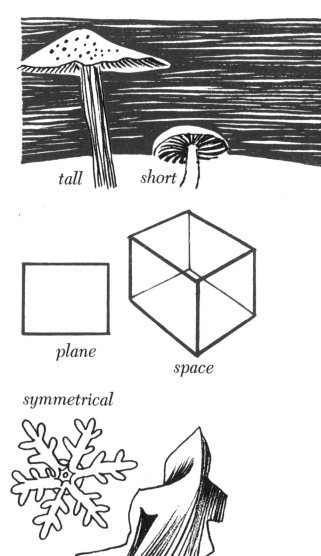

tall   *short*

plane   *space*

symmetrical

not-symmetrical

WHAT DOES THAT MEAN?

All snowflakes have symmetry.

Most rocks do not.

A square has symmetry.

A spiral does not.

A butterfly has symmetry.

A plant may not.

When a shape has symmetry, its design is
repeated on either side of a central dividing
line,
like this,
or this,   or this,

or this,

or this.

WHAT DO YOU THINK?

Would the house have sym-
metry if you added a
chimney on one side?
Do people have symmetry
in every direction?

To have symmetry, a shape does not have to match in every direction. Your head is symmetrical this way,

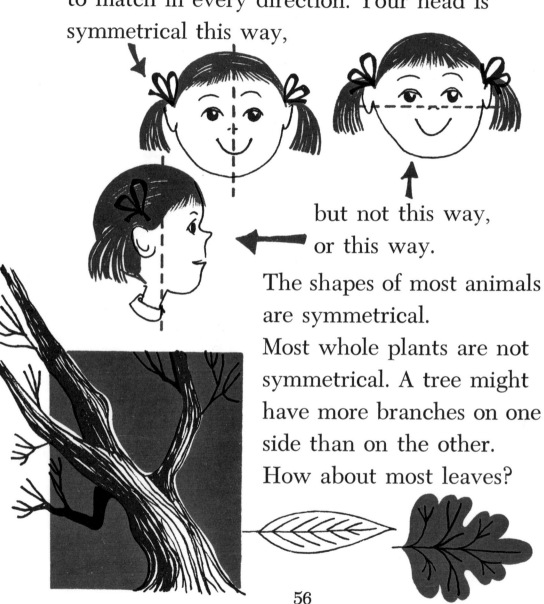

but not this way, or this way.

The shapes of most animals are symmetrical.

Most whole plants are not symmetrical. A tree might have more branches on one side than on the other. How about most leaves?

A plane figure is symmetrical if it can be folded so that one side fits exactly over the other.

What do you think about these?

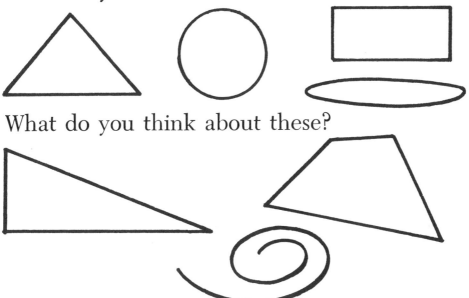

What do you think about these?

Can you name any shapes that are symmetrical in every direction?

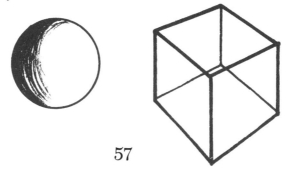

On these pages, how many things can you
see that are symmetrical?

How many things can you see that are not
symmetrical?

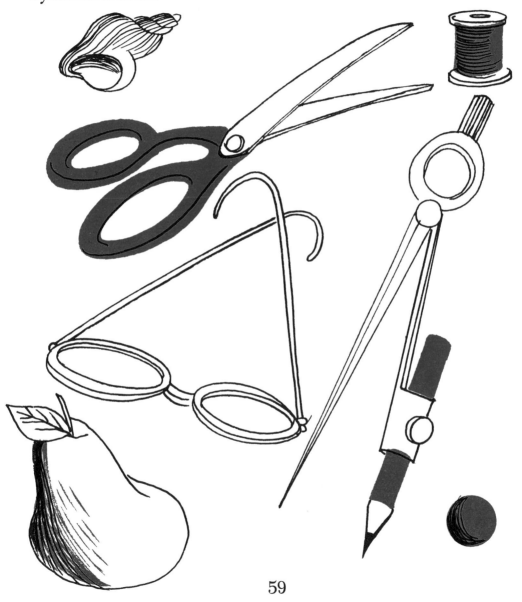

Whether a shape is symmetrical or not symmetrical,
it is a good shape if it works well.
Most living things are shaped right for their ways of living.
A bird's wings are shaped for soaring through the air — for sailing on the wind.

Fast-swimming sea creatures are shaped for slipping through the water.

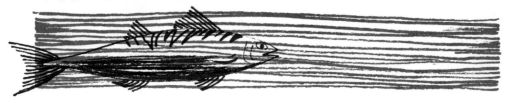

A tree is shaped so that sunlight falls on every green leaf.

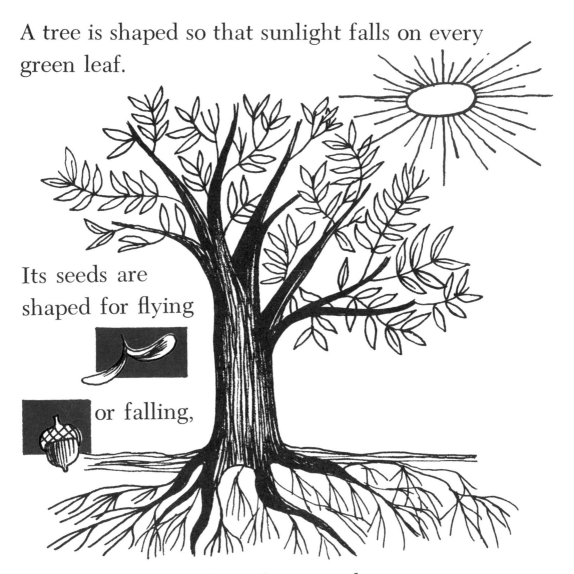

Its seeds are shaped for flying

or falling,

and its roots are shaped to get the most water from the earth.

Nature makes every kind of shape you can imagine —

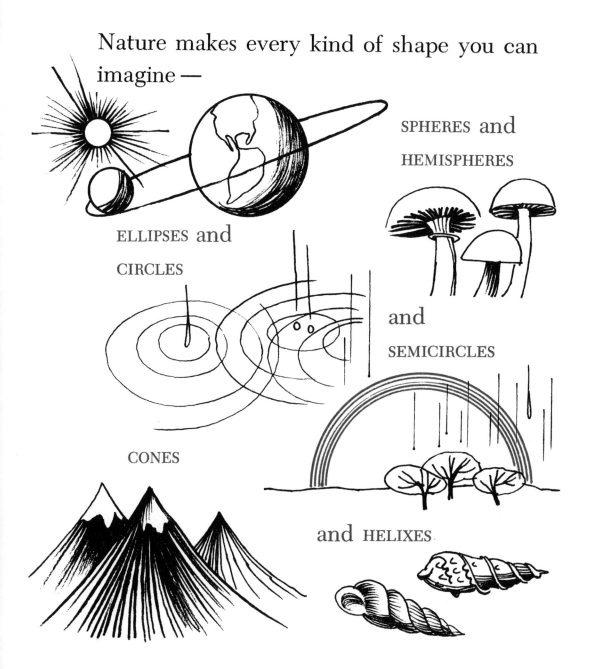

SPHERES and HEMISPHERES

ELLIPSES and CIRCLES

and SEMICIRCLES

CONES

and HELIXES

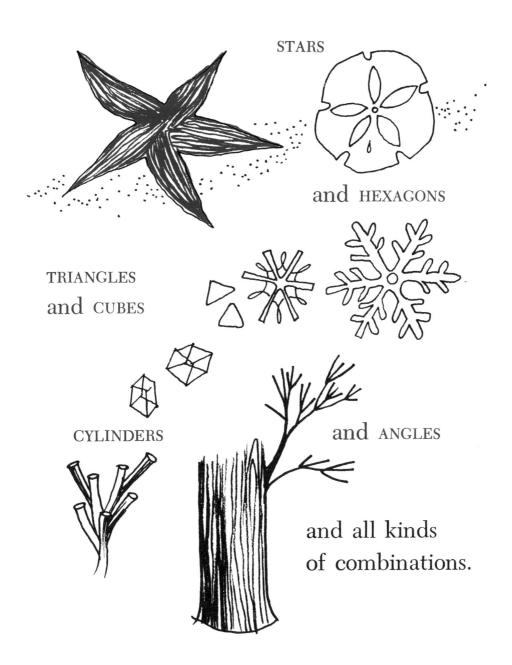

STARS

and HEXAGONS

TRIANGLES
and CUBES

CYLINDERS

and ANGLES

and all kinds
of combinations.

People build all kinds of shapes.
They build
CUBES (and other boxes),
PYRAMIDS,

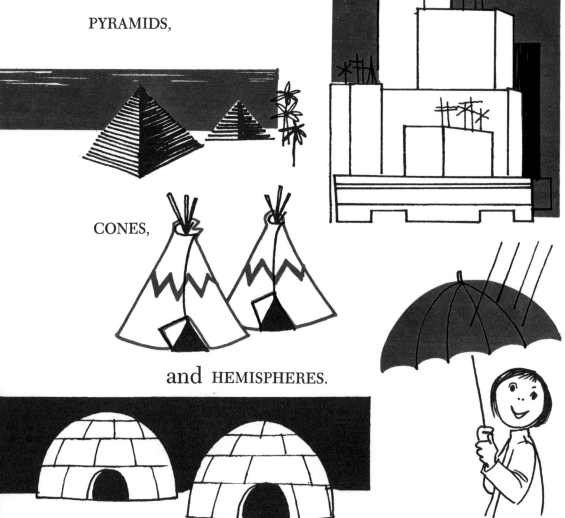

CONES,

and HEMISPHERES.

They make

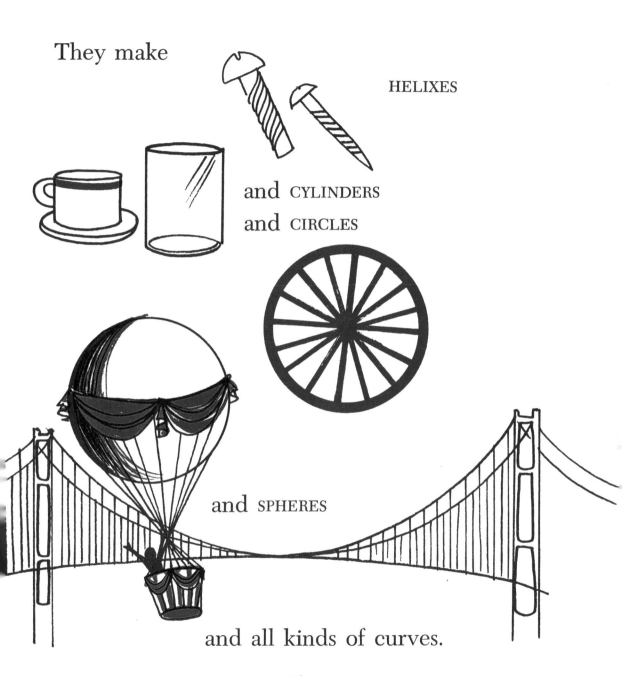

HELIXES

and CYLINDERS

and CIRCLES

and SPHERES

and all kinds of curves.

65

Shapes are for telling things. They can tell things without words. Shapes are for building with.

Shapes are for doing work. The round shape of a wheel, whether it is in a watch or on a truck or in part of a pulley is a shape at work.

Shapes are for enjoying. Everywhere you look you see beautiful shapes and interesting shapes.

Shapes are for imagining with. Can you imagine a new kind of shape? Can you imagine a shape with four dimensions?

INDEX